First published in 2007 by
Black & White Publishing Ltd
99 Giles Street, Edinburgh, EH6 6BZ
www.blackandwhitepublishing.com

Created and produced by The Foundry
Crabtree Hall, Crabtree Lane, Fulham,
London SW6 6TY, United Kingdom
www.foundry.co.uk

07 09 11 10 08

1 3 5 7 9 10 8 6 4 2

The Foundry is part of
The Foundry Creative Media Company Limited

ISBN: 978 1 84502 183 2

Printed in China

Thanks to: Cat Emslie, Victoria Lyle and Nick Wells

Life is Sweet

Ulysses Brave

BLACK & WHITE PUBLISHING

Foreword

Many years ago, I specialised in the observations of an eternity. Drawing inspiration from the natural world I found that the eternal secrets of the ancients are often reflected in our most intimate and mundane moments. Here are my most recent offerings of intuitive mortality.

Ulysses Brave

Sometimes the group focus can be misguided. If you think there is nothing to see or do, say so!

Always live in hope.

*If you are the object of
undying loyalty, remember
to use it wisely.*

Standing out in a crowd
is not always easy, try to
think big thoughts and
puff yourself up.

Striking out on your own can bring benefits, as long as you know where to find them.

Eagerness can be an endearing quality, although self-awareness is important too.

Focus on your goals, do not be put off by the fluffy, undirected attitudes of others.

Looking gorgeous can have its downsides. A wet nose for instance is not always appropriate for social occasions.

Take a moment out of your day to reflect on the simple successes of your life.

Excessive desire for ownership can lead to unpleasant arguments.

*Simple pleasures are
always the best.*

Studying meditation requires hours of practice every day. Once you have mastered the stillness you can remain silent for days.

Daydreaming is a useful method of allowing the brain to settle difficult issues. Try not to use it too often though.

*If you can't see
the way forward,
just wait until
the wind blows.*

Sometimes a good lie-down will sort out all of those irritating everyday problems.

Sometimes patience is required
to face the greatest challenges.

Our daily actions are constant reflections of the ancient mechanics of the stars.

Leaping into the unknown can
produce unexpected benefits.
Sometimes, not leaping at
all can be even better.

It is normal for children to challenge your authority from an early age. Try to maintain a cheerful disposition.

It is said that one's ears burn
when others talk about you.
Try not to let them talk
for too long.

*Value privacy above
self-aggrandisement.*

Try to look perky in the mornings, but also make sure you look in the mirror to check the effect is to your liking.

Sometimes it is worth struggling for love. If you win too easily, it is easy to lose it too.

Choose your friends wisely.

*If you're feeling a little fed-up,
try lifting yourself out of bed
one limb at a time.*

*Getting into shape is a
question of mind over
matter. You do not have to
be influenced by those
around you.*

*If you take a lead, others
will follow.*

Try to make friends with
your neighbours.

*A different perspective
on the world can provide
valuable insights.*

Always seek your inner beauty in the stillness of the moment. The longer the moment, the greater the beauty.

Hunting from a very early age
is not strictly necessary in our
modern, civilised society.

The whisper of eternal thoughts can come from the most unexpected sources.

Those first steps in life can be the most critical. As you grow older, you will encounter many different first steps.

See you soon ...